W9-AUI-505

75 FUN THINGS
to Make & Do by Yourself

75 FUN THINGS
to Make & Do by Yourself

Karen Gray Ruelle

Illustrated by Sandy Haight

 Sterling Publishing Co., Inc.   New York

Edited by Jeanette Green
Designed by Judy Morgan

Library of Congress Cataloging-in-Publication Data

Ruelle, Karen Gray.
    75 fun things to make & do by yourself / by Karen Gray Ruelle :
illustrated by Sandy Haight.
        p.   cm.
    Includes index.
    Summary: Crafts and activities divided into three categories
(noise-makers, stuff to do outside, and stuff to do inside) and
ranging from water-drop mouth noise to walking on the ceiling.
    ISBN 0-8069-0331-7
    1. Handicraft—Juvenile literature. [1. Handicraft.]
I. Haight, Sandy, ill. II. Title. III. Title: Seventy-five fun
things to make & do by yourself.
TT160.R84   1993
745.5—dc20   93-5091
                                          CIP
                                          AC

745.5
Ruel
c. 10
14.95

2 4 6 8 10 9 7 5 3 1

First paperback edition published in 1995 by
Sterling Publishing Company, Inc.
387 Park Avenue South, New York, N.Y. 10016
© 1993 by Karen Gray Ruelle
Distributed in Canada by Sterling Publishing
% Canadian Manda Group, P.O. Box 920, Station U
Toronto, Ontario, Canada M8Z 5P9
Distributed in Great Britain and Europe by Cassell PLC
Villiers House, 41/47 Strand, London WC2N 5JE, England
Distributed in Australia by Capricorn Link (Australia) Pty Ltd.
P.O. Box 6651, Baulkham Hills, Business Centre, NSW 2153, Australia
Manufactured in the United States of America

Sterling ISBN 0-8069-0331-7 Trade
0-8069-0332-5 Paper

Acknowledgments

With thanks to Steve and Susie, who started it; Sheila, who recognized it; Jeanette, who edited it; Lee, who encouraged it; and Nina, who will enjoy it. And thanks, most of all, to my mom and dad, who have always inspired a playful outlook.

CAUTIONARY NOTE TO PARENTS AND TEACHERS

No kid is 100 percent neat or 100 percent clean. Not many of the projects in this book promote these two admirable qualities. It is my hope that, instead, the projects encourage healthy curiosity, self-reliance and, most of all, a sense of fun.

Most of these projects are harmless—after all, how dangerous can a straw-wrapper spider be—but some do assume a certain amount of common sense. If you feel that your child is not handy with scissors and penknife, or that a project involving a lighted candle or edible rose-petals could be asking for trouble, you might want to peruse these projects before handing them over. Some parental supervision might be advised for certain sections. I've tried to indicate places where this could be the case, but really a parent or teacher is the best judge of a child's abilities.

Contents

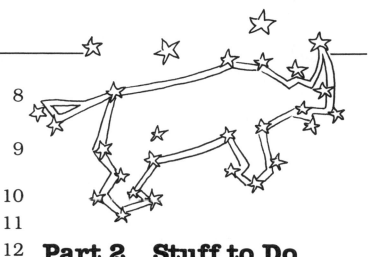

Introduction

BEING ON YOUR OWN can be lots of fun. When there's nobody else around, you can do what you like, when you like, any way you like. Nobody can boss you around and nobody can bother you.

The projects in this book are all things you can do when you're by yourself. Some involve a little mischief or messiness, so you might want to get an adult's OK. Many of them you can also do when it feels like you're by yourself. If you're the only kid in a house full of adults, or if you're stuck at a boring dinner party with your parents and their friends who just talk, talk, talk, and ignore you, try out some of these projects.

I learned how to walk on the ceiling when I was visiting my grandparents, and my brother and cousins were all too busy talking about baseball to pay any attention to me. When I was home sick from school, I invented the house of cards "trick."

If you follow the directions carefully, each of the activities and creations in this book will work for you. After a little practice, you can experiment with your own variations and maybe come up with even better ways of doing them. Then, later, if you like, you can show friends what you've been doing, and maybe they'll want to try out some of these projects, too.

Almost all the materials you'll need are probably around the house or outside in the yard. Just pick a project that sounds like fun, read the whole thing to make sure you understand all the steps, and then collect your materials.

If you live in an apartment, you may have to go to a park for some stuff, like twigs, acorns, or maple keys. If it's winter, you'll have to wait a few months to make rose-petal candy or daisy chains. But you're sure to find a project or two that you like.

Enjoy making noise, exploring, and creating. Have fun finding crazy constellations, drawing treasure maps, making straw-wrapper spiders, and walking on the ceiling!

Karen Gray Ruelle

PART 1 NOISEMAKERS

IT'S GREAT FUN TO make noise—the louder, the better. If you follow directions for these noise-making projects, you'll be able to tell everyone you're actually making music. That way, they won't be able to tell you to "quit making so much noise!"

You can play some noisemakers, like the glass harmonica, while waiting to be excused from the dinner table. You're not really alone, but it sometimes feels that way while you wait for others to finish eating.

For the water-drop mouth noise, like a few other noisemakers here, you won't need any equipment. Just practice in the back seat of the car during long trips, until you get it right. Your folks may look back to try to find the noisy leak!

The best thing about noisemakers is that if you practice enough, you can play tunes and beat out rhythms. You'll be able to play many, many songs once you get the hang of it. Or you can make up your own songs. Then, later, you can teach your friends to play, too. You could form a little band with Lee on bottle flute, Steve on the comb kazoo, and Susie on percussion with spoon castanets.

Whistling through a Blade of Grass

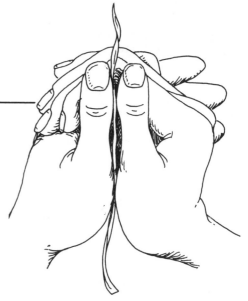

Whistling through a blade of grass is a little like whistling through your lips. Either you succeed on your first try or it takes a while, but suddenly works.

Pick a blade of grass—a wide one from a field or at the edge of a fence where nobody trims or mows. Make sure it's about three inches long or longer. Place your thumbs side by side, with the blade flat, running between your thumb knuckles. Then, cup your hands and bend your thumb tops over them. And blow through your thumb knuckles and the grass.

Experiment with the shape your cupped hands make and with the space at the pinkie end, until you get a whistle. If you practice, you can get a great, full sound.

Some people can whistle through a blade of grass without even using grass at all. All you have to do is hold your hands together the same way you did with the grass blade. Make sure your hands touch all around and you leave no holes where the air can come through, but leave a little hole at the bottom. You may have to practice to get it just right.

Strings

COMB KAZOO

A kazoo is a musical instrument that you can hum or sing through to make music. They sell little plastic ones at the store, but you can make your own out of a comb and a piece of waxed paper.

Take the waxed paper and wrap it once over the top of the comb. Then hold the waxed paper tight against the comb with your hands on each end. Place it up to your mouth, press your lips against the paper, and hum through the teeth of the comb. You'll have to hum loudly, almost like tooting. Toot any song you know. The sound will come out with a vibrating noise that's really funny.

This seems to work best when you toot through the wide-spaced comb teeth, and the louder you toot, the better it sounds.

RUBBER-BAND BASS GUITAR

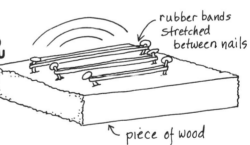

rubber bands stretched between nails

piece of wood

For this, you need something to stretch a rubber band across. Those old-fashioned cigar boxes work great if you take the lid off. But, you can use any other small box, or have an adult pound a few nails into a piece of wood and use that.

Anyway, stretch the rubber band around the box or between the nails. Then pluck the rubber band, and you'll get a twang. The tighter you stretch the rubber band the higher the twang. You can wrap the rubber band around more than once to make it more taut. You can have just one rubber band "string" to strum a bass line or several to pluck out a tune.

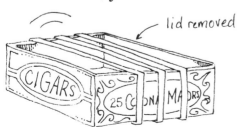

lid removed

CIGARS

Glass Works

BOTTLE FLUTE

This is fun to do since you have to drink a bottle of soda pop or juice first. After you've drunk it, you can use the bottle as a flute. Blow across and down into the hole. You can actually start this when there is still some liquid in the bottle, because the level of the liquid affects the sound. Drink and then blow different notes, as you go.

Put your bottom lip up against the near edge of the hole, push your upper lip out a little, over the top of the hole. Make an "O" shape with your lips; then blow out a steady stream of air. Experiment with how far you stick out your upper lip (pull it back and forth a little until you get it right), how round you

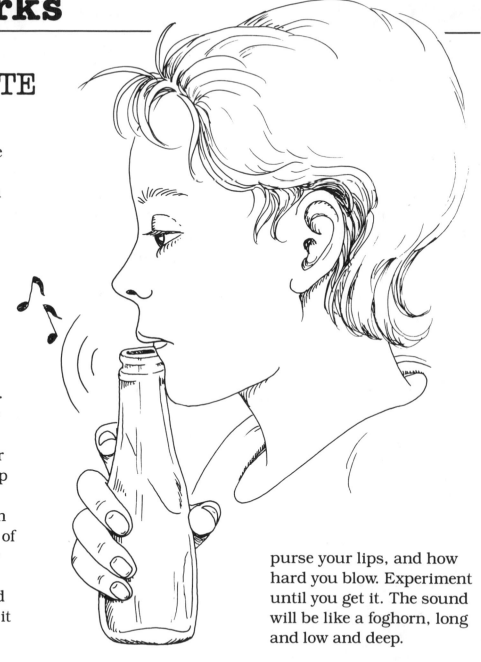

purse your lips, and how hard you blow. Experiment until you get it. The sound will be like a foghorn, long and low and deep.

GLASS HARMONICA

Here's a great noise you can make at the table. Of course, you can also do it elsewhere, but you'll need a glass. This works best with a really good wine glass, but try the less expensive kind, or your folks may not let you eat with them again! It's great for when you're bored with all the table talk when you have company. You'll need your parents' OK. They might even join you.

Hold your glass at the bottom with one hand to keep it from tipping over. Then, wet the index finger of your other hand, and lightly rub the tip of your wet finger around and around on the glass rim. Don't press too hard at first, just concentrate on keeping even pressure lightly round and round. After a while, increase the pressure slightly, and you'll hear a high-pitched hum from the glass. The hum will increase with your pressure and speed. As soon as the wet finger dries, the hum dies, so you'll have to stop once in awhile to re-wet your finger.

Each glass makes a slightly different sound. If you vary the amount of liquid in the glass, that changes the sound or note, too.

You could try different levels of liquid in several different glasses, until you get the notes you like. Play a simple tune by going from glass to glass.

Percussion

SPOON CASTANETS

If you want accompaniment when you're singing or making noise, try spoon castanets. Hold two spoons so that their rounded parts face each other. One spoon will rest between your thumb and the knuckle of your first finger. The other spoon will rest between your first and second fingers. Then, hit them against your thigh so that they smack each other.

It takes awhile to keep the spoons from swerving everywhere. But once you learn how, spoons are great for keeping the beat.

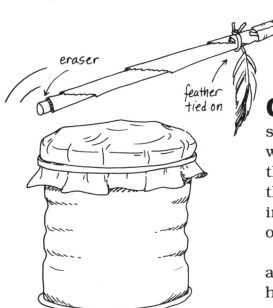

eraser

feather tied on

paper feather taped on

TIN CAN DRUM

Cans are good for lots of stuff. You can cover them with papier-mâché, paint the outside, and keep things inside; make them into melon-seed maracas; or make them into drums.

Use any size can to make a drum. If it's a can that has a plastic lid, like a coffee or shortening can, just wash it out and use it as is. If the can has no plastic lid, you have to make a top.

To make a top, lay waxed paper over the open end of the can, and secure it with a rubber band so that it's nice and taut. You now have a can drum.

For drumsticks, use the

eraser ends of pencils. Don't hit too hard or you might tear the waxed paper.

For decoration, tie feathers onto the ends of your drumsticks. Or cut some out of construction paper. Try covering the pencils with tinfoil first, then no one will know they're pencils.

You can also make a drum out of a glass jar, plastic container, or rounded Quaker Oats box. You *could* drum on the bottom of the can or container. That way you don't have to worry about breaking the waxed paper if you drum too hard. Try making a few drums and listening to the different sounds you get from each one.

MELON-SEED MARACA

Remember when you help fix dinner, and you need to scoop out all the stringy stuff with the seeds attached from a melon. Well, next time, save the seeds. Pick them out of the stringy pulp, wash them off, and let them dry. Spread them out on a paper towel and leave them overnight. Put the dried seeds inside a box or other container and shake vigorously. You've made a melon-seed maraca.

Try a shoebox or a smaller box. Tape the top on after you've put the seeds in, so they don't fly out. You can also use a frozen juice container with a lid that pops off. If the lid is missing, tape paper over the top or use a rubber band. You can also use a glass or plastic jar, like those used for spices or parmesan cheese. You could even use a small paper bag. Blow air into the bag and put in the seeds. Then twist the end shut tight, and wrap

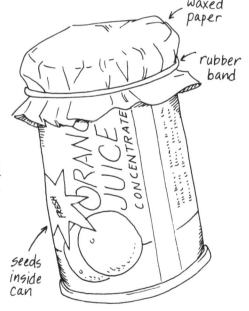

string or tape around it.

Seeds from winter squash or pumpkin, dried beans or buttons also work.

Water-Drop Mouth Noise

This is one of those things my brother could do and I just couldn't get it right. I practiced for hours until my cheek was sore. I then could still only do it sometimes. But when it works, it sounds great!

Use your thumb to snap the end of your finger (the nail side) against your cheek. That part is easy. The hard part is coordinating this snap with all the things you have to do with your mouth at the same time: Purse your lips like you're about to whistle. As you hit your cheek, push your tongue forward a little and expel air out of your mouth by kind of whistling, as though you're trying to say "VWIT" with just your lips.

If you get all this just right, the sound echoes when you snap your finger against your cheek. And it comes out sounding exactly like a cartoon version of a drop of water.

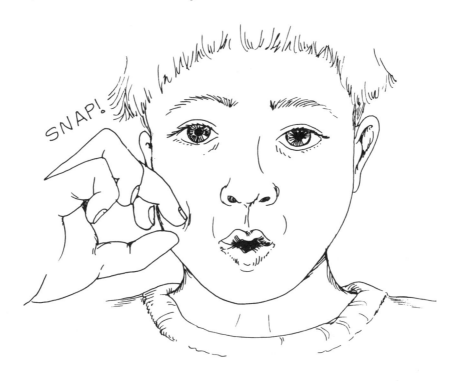

SNAP!

PART 2   STUFF TO DO OUTSIDE

WHENEVER YOU GO TO your favorite place outside, be on the lookout for things you can use for play in some other place or on some other day.

John is always on the lookout for skipping stones. When he throws one, the stone zings across the water so fast you can barely count the skips fast enough. I once saw a pebble skip thirteen times! But John has had lots of practice skipping stones for hours by himself. Well, maybe his dog Argo was with him.

Sometimes John discovered a lake or a beach where every stone was just right for skipping. At the lake near his house, the water was often perfectly smooth, but there wasn't a flat stone in sight. That's when he'd be happy he'd brought a bunch of stones in his pockets from his collection.

Seaweed Poppers

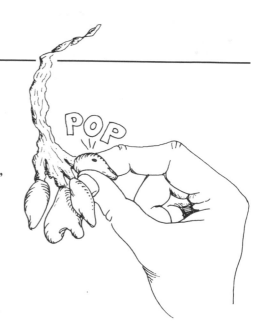

Seaweed poppers are really noisemakers from outside. At the beach, especially when the tide goes out, look along the water's edge for brownish green seaweed with little air-filled bubbles. The bubbles make a great pop when you squeeze them between your fingers.

This only works well when they're still wet. If you find dried black ones, they'll just crack disappointingly. Seaweed poppers work just like plastic bubble wrap that you get in packing cases: POP! POP! POP! POP!

OTHER BEACH STUFF

Look for those little air holes in the wet sand. Little clams and crabs under the sand make them.

When you step on wet sand, your footprint dries the sand slightly, and you can watch the sand dry in a patch around your foot as you step down. Then, when you step away, a wave may come in and completely erase your footprint.

Also, check out the footprints of seagulls and other birds. As the birds run faster and faster along the sand, ready to take off, their footprints become smaller and smaller. Last you'll see just the toes. Horseshoe crabs make neat tracks, too. Look for where they dragged a long tail along the sand. Also, sea grasses scratch the sand in

perfect circles around themselves as the wind blows. In the morning, you may even see deer prints or prints from other animals that have come during the night.

Shells with holes in them make good bracelets and necklaces. Just thread string through the holes and tie the ends together. Some thinner shells are translucent. Hold them

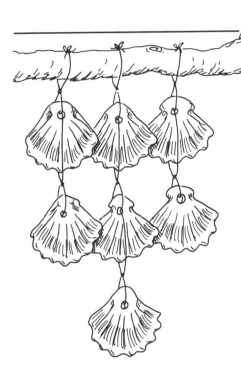

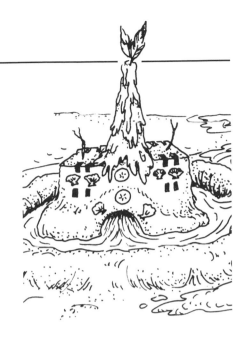

up and the light comes through. Poke a hole through them with a strong needle and string them into a nice necklace. You can also string a whole bunch of shells side by side on a stick to make a great windchime.

Sea glass is fun to collect, too. Water wears down the jagged edges of discarded glass from bottles and jars, until you have smooth, rounded, bright little pieces of glass. Keep them in a bowl on a windowsill so that light shines through them like a stained-glass window.

You'll find all sorts of great stuff at the beach— starfish, crabs inside abandoned shells, and jellyfish, yuck!

You can see right through the little round jellyfish that sometimes has little pink threads. They look like they're made of Jell-o, but they're much more solid. The ones with long tentacles can sting you, even after they're dead. Don't touch them!

You can build fantastic sandcastles, using shells and seaweed to adorn them. Take wet handfuls of sand, and drip the sand into mounds to make snazzy turrets or spires. Dig a moat around the castle, and watch it fill up as the tide comes in.

I liked to build sand animals. Once I made a huge turtle with shells all over his back and seaglass eyes. When the tide came in, it looked as though he were swimming out to sea.

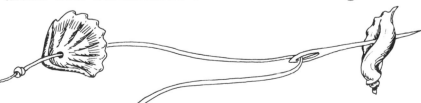

Autumn Leaves

My very favorite thing to do in autumn is to rake together a big pile of leaves and jump in them. Afterwards, you can kick the leaves along or watch the wind blow them away. You might see some really pretty ones you want to save.

GOING SOUTH

Look up at the sky and you might see a flock of birds, geese, or ducks flying South for the winter. They usually fly in a *V* shape, and usually one arm of the V is longer than the other. You may even hear geese honking.

JUST NUTS!

Squirrels and chipmunks scurry around, collecting nuts to store for winter. Sometimes they bury them or hide them in tree hollows. When I feed them peanuts, they usually eat the first one, bury the next one, and eat the third, bury the fourth, and so on. They bury each in a different place, when they think you're not watching. I don't know how they remember where all those nuts are. Maybe they use birch bark maps!

Fall Stuff

JACK-O'-LANTERNS

Autumn is pumpkin season, and Halloween is the best time to make a jack-o'-lantern. Paint or draw a face on the pumpkin with tempera paints or magic markers. Then, later, get a grown-up to cut off the pumpkin's top so that you can scoop out the goop inside. You can do this indoors if you want, but it's pretty messy. So, outside is probably best.

After you scoop out all the pumpkin goop, your grown-up could carve out the face you've drawn and help you put in a candle.

PUMPKIN SEEDS AND FLESH

Don't forget to keep the pumpkin seeds for roasting and eating or for making a melon-seed necklace. To roast the seeds, first rinse off all the pumpkin goop. Then spread out the seeds on a cookie sheet, and sprinkle a little salt over them. Get a grown-up to set the oven at 350 degrees F (175 degrees C) and roast them for 15 minutes. When they're cool, split each open with your teeth and eat the seed inside.

Pumpkin flesh is edible, too. You could buy two pumpkins. Make one into a jack-o'-lantern and find a good cook to make the second one into pumpkin pie or pumpkin bread!

Snow and Winter Stuff

A snowy day is full of possibilities. Catch snowflakes on your tongue and taste the winter. Scoop up clean, newly fallen snow into a paper cup. Then pour a little juice, honey, chocolate syrup, or maple syrup over it for a real snow treat. Use a spoon to stir in the flavoring. Then slurp it up!

Everyone knows how to make snowballs. Try setting up targets like a hat on top of a mound of snow or a mitten waving from a stick. Or just aim at the middle of a large tree trunk to perfect your aim for snowball fights later on.

SNOW ANGELS

Fall backwards into the snow. Then flatten the snow around you by flapping your arms up and down and moving your legs together and apart. Your impression will look like an angel with wings and a long gown. Get up carefully and take a look.

WACKY FOOTPRINTS

After a snowstorm you can make wacky footprints. There are ones that lead nowhere and ones that do impossible things. To make baffling footprints that lead nowhere, pick a place with lots of fresh snow and start walking. Make your footprints clear and deep. Walk for awhile, then stop. Now walk backwards, stepping carefully into the footprints you made when you were walking forward. Then inspect your work!

Try other impossible things, like walking around a tree with one foot on one side and the other foot on the tree's other side. Hop around the tree's right side on your right foot, then hop backwards around the other side on your left foot. Then, carefully hop forward again, into your own footprints, and continue walking.

LOOK FOR ANIMAL TRACKS

In the country, you can find deer, bird, squirrel, and rabbit tracks, and sometimes raccoon and fox tracks, too. If you're lucky, bigger animals may have left their tracks. In the city, you can find bird, squirrel, dog, cat, and sometimes mouse and rat tracks. Of course, you'll see all sorts of people tracks. Try to identify animals by the shape and size of their tracks. Library books can help.

SNOW POURRI

After a snowfall, find a big tree—pines work great—stand under a long branch, grab it, and shake it as hard as you can. You'll give yourself a snow shower.

Take a water pistol and shoot a melting message in the snow. Breathe hot breath onto a cold window or mirror and draw on it with your finger. Draw

pictures in the frost, or leave messages on snowy windshields of parked cars.

If it's really windy, you can fly on ice. Put on a cape or long coat, or wrap a blanket around you. Stand on the ice, then hold your coat open so that it catches the wind like a sail. You can fly even faster if you wear your ice skates. Just don't skate on any thin ice! Ask an adult if it's safe.

From the bank, look for stuff frozen into the ice of ponds: sticks, leaves, snakes in frozen, curving zigzags.

Building things in the snow is wonderful to do in the winter. A snow fort can be built from piled up snow, with a doorway dug into it, surrounded by walls for extra protection from the enemy. Or try building an igloo by cutting bricks out of crusty snow. Use the edge of your hand or a stick. Then pile up the snow bricks into a round wall, sloping it inward as you build it up. Lay in a good supply of snowballs for the big battle.

Snowmen are fun to make, but you don't have to make just snowmen. You can build snowwomen, snow animals, snow cars, snow monsters, even snow space ships. You name it. Use whatever you can find for accessories—sticks for arms or control levers, pebbles for eyes or dashboard switches, leaves for hair, pine needles for whiskers, twigs for monster teeth.

And when you're tired and cold, go indoors for a cup of hot cocoa, and check out Stuff To Do Inside.

slice a round brick of packed, icy snow

entrance

Spring Bugs

When spring arrives, days grow longer, and that means more time to play outside. As the snow melts, you sometimes get little rushing rivers in the gutters. They're fun to watch, but stay on the sidewalk away from cars.

In spring, everything starts to grow again. Look for tiny buds on the trees, as well as crocuses, daffodils, and grass poking up through the dirt.

Pick up rocks to see what's underneath. Sometimes you find all sorts of bugs and worms. Try kicking or using a rock to pound open a rotting log to see inside.

Bugs also skim along the surface of ponds. Look for tadpoles and other small fish. Later, when the tadpoles grow into frogs, try to spot them hopping and splashing in ponds and streams or sunning themselves on nearby rocks. Since they blend in with their surroundings and often stay perfectly still, it's hard to find them.

Skipping Stones

Next time you're at the beach or by a lake or pond, try skipping stones. It works best when the water is calm. Find as many smooth, flat stones as you can.

Face the water, and hold the stone in your hand with its flat side level with the ground. Use your thumb and forefinger, bend your elbow and twist your wrist so that your hand is close

to your body. Spin the stone out in a smooth motion as you unfold your hand and elbow, always keeping the stone's flat side level with the ground. At the end of the spin, release the stone so that it continues to spin as it is hurled out over the water. When it hits the water's surface, it will bounce into the air and land again and again, skipping across the water's surface. See how many skips you can get in one throw.

Before you skip any stones, make sure no one is in the water who might get hurt. This really is fun to do when you're alone. Collect a bunch of stones for next time. Just keep some in your pocket for when you find a pond.

Rubber Bands

RUBBER-BAND BALL

My Grandmother Cyd saved everything from string, shopping bags, and candles to wrapping paper, ribbon, and rubber bands. She kept most of her junk in a kitchen drawer, but she stored rubber bands on doorknobs all over her apartment. She taught me how to make a rubber-band ball.

For a rubber-band ball, you need lots of rubber bands. So keep saving them until you have enough. My grandmother saved hundreds! Then, take a small piece of paper or cardboard, folded up tiny, and begin by wrapping a rubber band around the paper. Then twist the rubber band, wrap it back across, twist it again, and repeat until you use up the

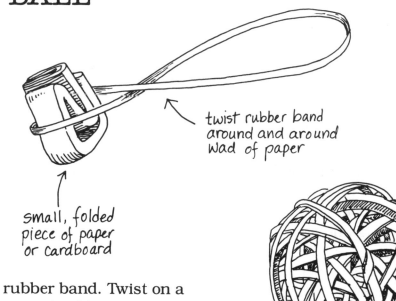

twist rubber band around and around wad of paper

small, folded piece of paper or cardboard

rubber band. Twist on a second rubber band, then a third and a fourth, and keep going until you've got a nice rubber-band ball.

Because it's uneven, the ball will bounce funny, going off into unexpected directions. Try setting up targets outside to see if you can hit them. Bounce the ball on the ground or against the side of a building and catch it. Try bouncing and

clapping your hands before you catch it. Or bounce the ball, spin around, and catch it. Make up your own variations or play a new version of jacks, by picking up acorns, leaves, stones, twigs, or bottle caps between bounces.

Paper Airplanes

To make a basic paper airplane, take a rectangular piece of paper, like typing paper or paper from a yellow pad. Use any paper you want, but make it into a rectangle first.

Fold the paper in half, the long way, with the fold at the bottom. Then, fold down two corners of one end for the nose. Fold down each side to make the wings.

To help with the weight and to get your plane to fly straight, put a paper clip on the nose. Open the wings. Throw the plane forward and up a little. If you have designed the plane well, it should catch an air current and fly in a nice line. You could create a chalk landing strip on a sidewalk. Or the plane could land between two bushes in a yard or park.

After you get the hang of it, experiment with fancy folds, cuts, and tears. These alterations will change the weight of the plane and the direction it will fly. Try turning down the nose a little to make your plane loop-the-loop. You can also decorate your plane with colors or a special design. You could even give it a name, just like they do with some war or stunt planes.

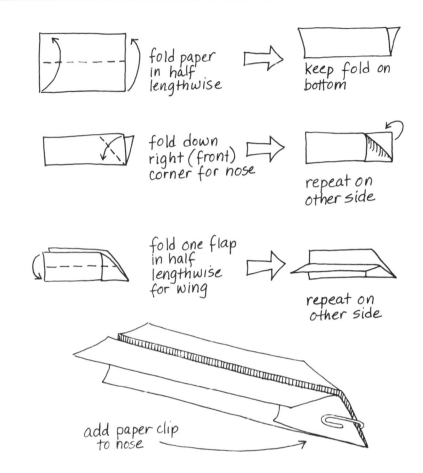

fold paper in half lengthwise

keep fold on bottom

fold down right (front) corner for nose

repeat on other side

fold one flap in half lengthwise for wing

repeat on other side

add paper clip to nose

Whirligigs and Rhino Noses

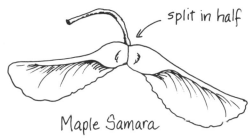

split in half

Maple Samara

In autumn, when leaves fall from the trees, you'll find little green things that look like wings held together by a stem.

These "maple keys" are flying seeds or samaras that come from maple trees.

Find a maple key and tear it in half along where the stem joins the two halves. Then tear off the stem. Hold one half high in the air, and let it go! The maple key flutters down in a spin like a whirligig. Try holding one up in each hand to see which one reaches the ground first. They flutter like crazy.

Take another maple key and tear it in half. Then split the thick end with your fingernail. It's kind of sticky inside. I think that's where the actual seed is.

You can also stick the maple key onto the bridge of your nose like a rhinoceros horn. Or try one on each ear, and you'll have long, dangly earrings. Or put one on each fingernail for a Fu Manchu or Dragon Lady look.

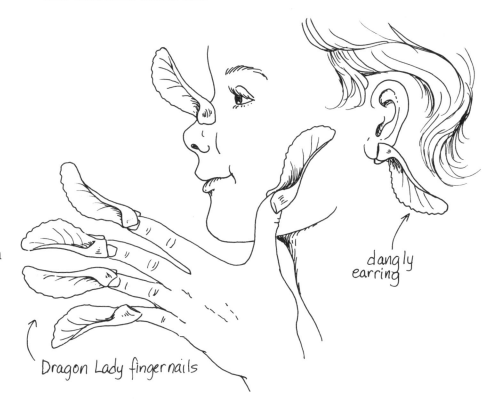

Dragon Lady fingernails

dangly earring

Flower and Leaf Chains

DAISY CHAINS AND CROWNS

For a chain or crown, pick about ten daisies. Make a small slit with your fingernail in the stem of the flower about halfway down. Then thread a second stem through the slit all the way to the base of the flower. Now make a slit in the second stem, and slip a third stem through that.

make slit with fingernail and slip stem through

Keep going until you have a chain long enough for a crown or a necklace. At the end, tie two stems together or make more slits and keep threading the ends through and wrapping them around each other until they hold fast. This also works with Queen Anne's Lace.

GREENSLEEVES

stem — Leaves fastened together with Stems

second chain of leaves fastened to first chain, etc.

You can also make necklaces, crowns, belts, and even clothing out of leaves. Here's how you put them together: Place two leaves end to end, overlapping them a bit. Then, thread a stem through the overlapping part from top to bottom and then to the top again. Add another leaf, and another, and another, and soon you'll have a chain long enough for a belt, crown, or necklace.

You can also fasten leaf chains to other leaf chains, side by side, in the same way. You can even make skirts, hats, shirts, capes, or anything you like.

Tree Rubbings

For this kind of nature drawing, you need paper that's not too thick. Typing paper, rice paper, or a torn and flattened paper bag will do. Construction paper is too thick and stiff. You also need something to draw with—pencils, charcoal, or crayons. Press the paper against the tree trunk—make sure you choose a bumpy one—and feel the bark's bumps and crevices. Rub lightly with the side of your pencil rather than the point. You end up with a picture or "rubbing" that shows the texture of the bark.

You can also make rubbings of brick walls, gravestones, manhole covers, and other things. Anything with a good, hard, textured, or raised surface works.

tack holding paper to tree

rubbing with side of crayon, charcoal, or pencil

SHADOW DRAWINGS

To make a shadow drawing, use any kind of paper or cardboard you like and a pencil, crayon, magic marker, or paint. Find nice shadows on the ground of leaves, branches, or other things, and place your paper underneath them to catch their shadows. Hold the paper in place with a rock on each corner. You can also use a wall. Simply fasten your paper onto the wall with tape or a thumbtack. Then, trace the shadow outlines on the paper. If

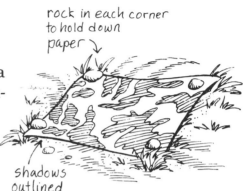

rock in each corner to hold down paper

shadows outlined

you forget what you're drawing and just concentrate on the shapes, you can end up with wonderful abstract drawings. You can color them in or even make nice presents or birthday cards.

SUNDIALS

To make a sundial, put a stick in the ground and hold paper under the stick's shadow. Draw the shadow, and wait for the shadow to move. Go away and come back later when the sun has moved a little in the sky. Then draw the new shadow. You can record how the shadow moves as the day progresses. This is how a sundial tells time.

You can make your own sundial by putting paper or cardboard on the ground. Then draw a big circle on the paper. To make a perfect circle, use a compass or trace around a big bowl or plate. Then drive a stick through the center of the circle. Now, mark where the stick's shadow falls at each hour, and note the time. The next day, place your sundial in exactly the same place and position, and you'll be able to tell time by seeing where the shadow falls.

Birch-Bark Treasure Maps

If you're in an area with lots of birch trees you can do some great stuff with the bark. Birch trees have smooth white bark with little horizontal lines through it that look like slashes.

Try this with bark from trees that have fallen down. Strip off some bark from a fallen tree. You'll find it peels right off. Then peel off the top layer of bark, so that the bark is very thin and its inside is tan. Peel it down as thin as you can, and you'll have a very flexible piece of birch bark.

Don't peel bark from living trees or you could harm the trees. You're bound to find lots of fallen trees with perfect bark— not too dry, but not too damp either.

In the Northeast United States, where I grew up,

Native American Indians used to draw maps on birch bark. You can do the same thing. Birch bark is perfect for drawing on, and it isn't brittle at all. You could even use a real quill pen to write with!

sharpened end with slit

QUILL PEN

A quill is the bottom of a feather that attaches the feather to the bird. Buy or wash a feather and let it dry. Use a pocketknife to sharpen it into a point, and then make a slit in the point, to help it soak up ink. Stick the point of your quill pen into gobs of crushed berries and write on the bark with ink or blueberry juice. Of course, you can use pens, crayons, charcoal, and all sorts of other things for writing on birch bark.

You could make up your own picture language to describe how to get to a certain spot in the woods, in your back yard, or even in your room. Bury or hide a small treasure—maybe a papier-mâché armband, melon-seed necklace, or perfect skipping stones. Keep the map to remind you how to find them later. Or give the treasure map to a friend.

BIRCH BARK AND OTHER BOATS

Birch bark also makes nice boats. Peel a good strip of bark, fold it in half, and close up the edges for a little canoe. Sew the edges with needle and thread. Or use a very thin green twig to close them by poking holes into the bark with a penknife or scissors. Then thread the twig through the holes to hold the ends together. Stiff weeds that look like wheat work well for this, too.

For another kind of boat, just poke the stem of a leaf into the leaf's other end to make it curl up. For a cork boat, stick a toothpick into a cork, and then put a leaf on the other end of the toothpick like a sail. Then you're ready to set sail. The cork boat will really bob and float.

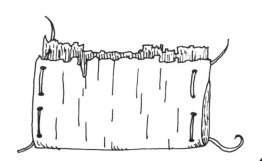

Birch Bark Boat

Cork Boat

Leaf Boat

POOHSTICKS

In A.A. Milne's book *The House at Pooh Corner* Winnie-the-Pooh and his friends play the game, "Poohsticks." You can play, too. Take two sticks or two boats you've made, drop both into a creek upstream. Then run downstream following them to see which one gets to a certain spot first.

This works well when you drop them into water on one side of a bridge, then rush to the other side of the bridge to see whose boat or stick wins. Mark your boats with colored leaves or other devices to tell them apart. Sometimes the boats will shoot downstream, and other times they'll get caught in an eddy and swirl around in one place.

Cloud Pictures

If you're in a dreamy mood, and it's the right kind of day, cloud watching can be fun. Get comfy—lying in a field, sprawled out on the lawn, or sitting by your window—and look up at the clouds, and imagine different shapes. I've found many animals in clouds—horses racing, bunnies hopping, fish floating, dragons roaring, elephants stomping. I've also found lots of funny-looking faces and some-times plane or boat shapes. Once I thought I saw the Wicked Witch of the East riding her bicycle across the sky.

When it's windy, clouds move and change shape more quickly, but on a calm day, they sometimes last a while before assuming another shape. It also looks pretty when the sun breaks through a cloud, and rays of sunlight stream to the ground. Dramatic events seem to unfold up there, like curtains parting to reveal great patches of blue and bright yellow sunlight.

Catching Fireflies

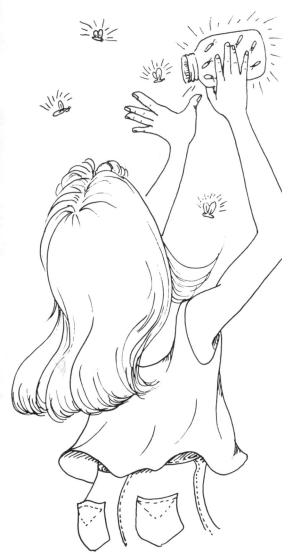

In summertime, as dusk falls, fireflies or "lightning bugs" come out. Their lights flash off and on as they fly. They may be hard to see at first. But when you're playing outside and it begins to get dark, you may see one light up, then another, and another one. Soon they're all over the place!

If you're quick, you might be able to catch them in a jar, and watch them light up the jar like a lantern. Screw on a lid with small perforations in it, or use waxed paper with pin holes so that the fireflies can breathe. Attach the waxed paper with a rubber band. But, be sure to let them go before you go home. Otherwise, they'll die in the jar overnight, and you'll wake up in the morning with a jar full of dull, dead bugs.

Star-Gazing

SHOOTING STARS

When you're exhausted from chasing fireflies, and you want to stay out just a little longer, it's fun to search the sky for shooting stars. It's easiest to see them outside in the country where there are few lights. But you can also watch from your window, if it's dark enough. Or slip outside on the porch or lawn and watch the sky.

"Shooting stars"—really meteor dust and particles —occur somewhere in the sky nearly every minute. But in an hour of sky watching, you probably won't see more than six.

The easiest way to find them is to choose a small section of sky to watch. A shooting star appears like a star falling from the sky that leaves a trail of light. This happens very fast; so, you might think you imagined it at first. Also, if you wear glasses, your lens may distort the light when you turn your head sideways. So, you may suppose you've seen one. But you'll know when you've *really* seen one. It's magical— make a wish!

During meteor showers, lots of shooting stars are visible. Then you'll double your chances of seeing some. Don't worry—you won't get wet! In the northeastern United States and Canada, you can see a major meteor shower in August, and in other parts of the world you may be able to see a meteor shower in the constellation Leo in mid-November. Check your local newspaper's weather section for news of meteor showers.

CRAZY CONSTELLATIONS

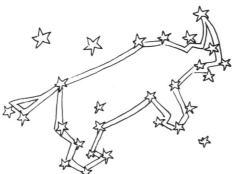

Stars seem to outline shapes. These different shapes or patterns are called constellations. Newspapers also highlight which ones you can see that night.

Many stories about star constellations come from Greek and Roman myths.

Other cultures, like Native American Indian and Eskimo, also have stories about the stars and the shapes they make. You can also make up your own crazy constellations, with your own stories behind them, like playing connect the dots with the stars. Try writing down the stories in your own star book, drawing your star constellations, and finding them again the next night.

Date: May 16
Time: 9:15 pm
Name of Constellation
  Barking Dog Star
Myth:
  This dog first appeared in the sky after it got tired of chasing the sky cat star.

PART 3 STUFF TO DO INSIDE

THERE'S NO SUCH thing as nothing to do. Not even when you're stuck inside on a rainy day, or when you have a cold and can't go out to play! Those times can be the most fun. Set up a house of cards, make a mask out of papier-mâché, or fold elaborate paper dolls and make them dance on your windowsill.

Even a meal with a bunch of grown-ups can be fun if you make a straw-wrapper spider or try out a mysterious balancing salt shaker. There's always something to do.

When you go with parents to visit relatives, you won't need to fidget, squirm, or complain. When you arrive, you'll be able to come up with something to do that's really fun. You'll soon forget that you'd thought you'd be bored or lonely. At my Grandmother Sally's house, I discovered how to walk on the ceiling!

Waxed Leaves and Flowers

Here's how to save leaves or flowers. Take leaves and flowers you like and place them between two pieces of waxed paper. Then, find two pieces of brown paper from a paper bag. Put the flower and waxed paper in between the brown paper, like a sandwich, then iron the whole thing so that it flattens out. Don't turn the iron on too high or it might burn! The waxed paper kind of melts together and encases the flowers or leaves, and the brown paper protects the iron and the ironing board from the melting waxed paper.

After you've pressed your flowers or leaves in waxed paper, hang them on a window. When the sun shines, light outlines the leaf and filters through the waxed paper, making it resemble a stained-glass window.

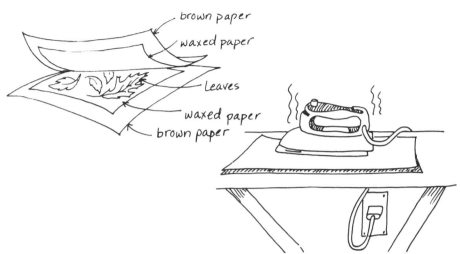

brown paper
waxed paper
Leaves
waxed paper
brown paper

PRESSED LEAVES AND FLOWERS

Or put a nice autumn leaf in the dictionary—under *L* for "leaf," *M* for "maple," or *S* for "sycamore"! After a few days, the book's weight will press the leaf flat. Of course, you can use any heavy book; you don't need a dictionary. This works well with daisies but not with roses or other thick flowers. It's also not really very good for the book.

That's because the chemicals in the flower or leaf set up a reaction with the paper and begin to stain. But it presses them well. You could put the leaf or flower between two sheets of typing paper inside the book to help prevent stains.

Rose-Petal Candy

To make rose-petal candy, make sure the roses you use have not been sprayed with insecticide or anything else. This means you probably shouldn't use flowers from a store or flower shop. Only use roses from your garden if you're absolutely sure they haven't been sprayed. If you're not positive, ask your folks, and if they're not sure, don't do it.

To make the candy, pull the petals off a rose, wash them gently in water, and lay them out on a paper towel to dry.

Separate an egg yolk— the yellow part—from the white. Crack the eggshell in half, carefully pour the yolk from one half to the other, back and forth. Let the egg white dribble out the sides into a bowl underneath. Be careful not to get any yolk into the bowl or this project might not work. Take the egg white, add a spoonful of water, and beat it with a fork or an egg beater until it gets frothy.

Next, dip each rose petal into the frothy egg white, pour a little sugar on each side, and lay out the petals on a pan or plate to dry in the sun. Even on a very hot day, it will take them several hours to dry. Sprinkle a little sugar in the pan before you place the petals on it to keep them from sticking to the pan.

When the petals are dry, you can eat them. They taste the way roses smell.

You can make candy out of other edible flowers this way, like violets and lavender. But be very sure that the flowers are indeed safe to eat, and use only the petals or the flower parts. Also make sure they have not been sprayed.

Separating an Egg

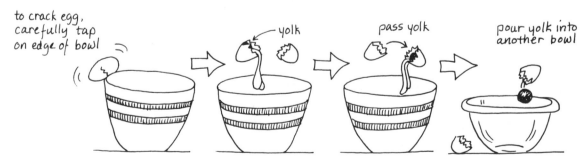

to crack egg, carefully tap on edge of bowl

yolk

pass yolk

pour yolk into another bowl

Simple Dyes

COFFEE PARCHMENT

If you want to make paper that looks like it's really old, here's how. Take any old white paper (typing paper works great) and lay it in a pan of coffee. Ask your parents for leftover coffee from the pot. The coffee doesn't have to be hot or fresh. Make sure the paper gets soaking wet with coffee and let it sit. I used to let it soak overnight, but a few hours might work. Experiment to see how dark you like it.

Then, take the paper out and let it dry. Use clothespins or paper clips to hang the paper on the line to dry, or just lay it on a paper bag or old newspaper. You can make treasure maps on this stuff. It really looks authentic, like the old paper called *parchment* that was

once used for important documents.

Use a quill pen dipped in ink to write on your coffee parchment. You'll have to keep dipping your quill pen into the ink, just like in the old days, before ballpoint pens and magic markers. Try writing with fancy letters on your coffee parchment to make it look real.

CELERY FLOWERS

Celery is good to eat plain or covered with peanut butter and raisins. It's also good to make into celery flowers.

You know all the stringy stuff in the celery? Well, that's the reason you can make celery flowers.

To make celery flowers, you need celery, food coloring, and small containers. Cups, glasses, or plastic containers are fine. Put water into several containers, and add a few drops of food coloring to each container. Choose a different color for each cup.

Wash the celery. Then, cut off a few stalks, leaving the leafy stuff at the top, and stand each stalk up in a cup of colored water, After about an hour, the color from the water begins to

color travels up veins and strings to flowery stuff on top

water with food coloring

yellow   red   blue

travel up the celery strings or veins and a few hours after that, leaves at the top change color. The celery looks like flowers.

After this little experiment, use the celery to decorate food or eat it.

Paper Creations

Paper is fun to make things out of. Origami is a Japanese paper-folding method for making animals and shapes. You can also cut things out of paper.

PAPER SNOWFLAKES

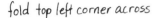
fold top left corner across

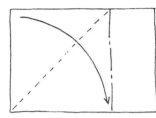

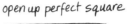
cut off this part

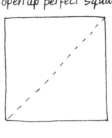

open up perfect square

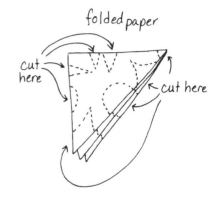
folded paper

cut here

cut here

One of the simplest paper cut-outs you can make is a paper snowflake. It also comes out really pretty. This works best with a square piece of paper. Fold the paper in half, then in half again, either as a triangle or a rectangle. Then cut bits out of the paper in any shape you want. When you unfold it, you'll have perfectly symmetrical shapes, cuts, and angles.

Hang your snowflake on the window to allow light to shine through the holes.

Paper snowflakes make great winter decorations. Just like real snowflakes, no two seem exactly alike. Try hanging some on your Christmas tree or over your bedroom doorway.

Colored paper is a nice touch. Or try drawing on the paper first, or glue sparkles on it before you cut. You can also cut snowflakes out of aluminum foil, but be careful when unfolding them so that they don't tear.

PAPER DOLLS

You can make a string of paper dolls by folding a long piece of paper back and forth like an accordion. Cut out the folded-up paper into the shape of a person, making sure you leave some folded paper uncut on each side, so they'll still be attached to each other when you unfold it. Color them in after you unfold them, if you like. Or you could color the paper first; then you'll have a surprise when you cut them out.

You don't have to cut out people. You can cut out a string of paper elephants, dogs, robots, houses, stars, or anything you like. It's completely up to you.

If you place the paper dolls on a smooth, flat surface (like a table top) and blow

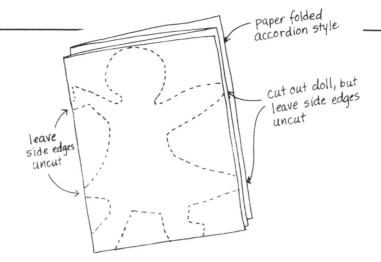

paper folded accordion style

cut out doll, but leave side edges uncut

leave side edges uncut

lightly at the bottom, they'll move forward or "dance." You could cut out a line of ballerinas and make a stage for them on your windowsill. Part the curtains and make them dance.

Newspaper

NEWSPAPER HAT

Once your family has finished reading the newspaper, you can do many things with the paper besides recycling it. Try making a newspaper hat. Printers wore these to keep the ink out of their hair in newspaper plants. Take one sheet of newspaper and fold it back along its natural fold. Then fold it in half the other way so that you have a fold at the top. Now fold down each of the two top corners to make a point in the middle of the top.

Then, fold up two layers of newspaper hanging off the bottom. Then turn the paper over and fold the other two layers up on the other side. You now have a newspaper hat. If it unfolds too easily, you can always tape it. You can also paint or color it, if you wish.

If the hat is too big, or you cannot get it to stay folded together, do this: Pull the middle of the bottom out on each side,

so the ends go down into two points, and flatten it that way. Then, fold up the two points, one on each side. You now have a smaller, sturdier news-

paper hat. You can repeat this step for an even smaller hat. Try making a bigger one for yourself and a smaller one for your doll or robot.

← fold horizontally

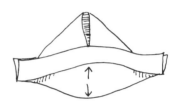
pull middle out on each side

fold newspaper back along its natural fold

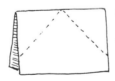
with last fold on top, fold down the top 2 corners to make a point in the middle

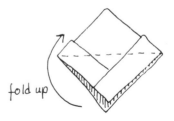
fold up

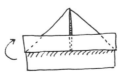
fold up layers of newspaper hanging from the bottom

NEWSPAPER STAFF

roll 2 sheets of newspaper together

cut slits into the top about 6 inches (15 cm) long

hold bottom

pull strips until you have a nice twisting flare of flapping strips

tape bottom to keep staff rolled tight

Shepherds, hikers, ancient monarchs, and church officials use staffs. To make one, take two sheets of newspaper, and lay one down on top of the other. Then roll them up, not too tightly and not too loosely. Hold onto the bottom to keep it rolled up. Cut slits into the top part, about 6 inches long.

Now comes the tricky part. Hold onto the bottom of the roll with one hand to keep it rolled up, and then grab some slitted paper strips in the center of the top with your other hand. Gently pull them up out of the center of the roll. You'll be pulling them around in a twist as they are pulled up. Keep a good grip on the bottom of the roll as you do this. Pull until you have a twisting flare of flapping strips that cover the top third of your staff.

If the bottom part unrolls a little, just pull it back tight, and maybe even tape the bottom and the middle a little to keep the staff rolled up. You can shake your newspaper staff and march around, looking official in your newspaper hat.

Fortune-Teller

All the kids in my school knew how to make a paper fortune-teller. We also called them cootie-catchers. (Cooties are lice!)

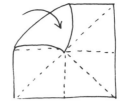
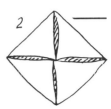

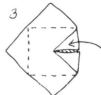

BASIC COOTIE-CATCHER

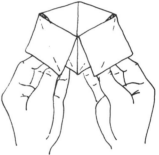

Fold a square of paper in half to make a triangle. Now fold it in half again to make a smaller triangle, and do this two more times. Open the paper up and fold each corner down into the middle, using the creases as guides, so that all four corners meet in the middle. Turn the paper over and do the same thing on the other side. Then, fold the paper in half, by folding the bottom up to the top, with the folded corners inside.

You now have a paper with folds on top and openings on the bottom. Put your forefingers and thumbs inside the bottom openings, with your left thumb and forefinger on the left side, and your right thumb and forefinger on the right side, with one thumb or finger inside each opening. Press your fingers and thumbs into the points, and then press all these points together toward the middle so that you push the paper together into one big point, where all the little points meet. As you do this, pop the corners of the paper out. Now you have a cootie-catcher.

If you move both forefingers at the same time, away from your thumbs, the cootie-catcher opens up one way. And then if you put them back together and then move your right forefinger and thumb away from your left forefinger and thumb, the cootie-catcher opens another way and exposes a different set of surfaces.

See if you can catch "cooties" or other small objects.

TELLING FORTUNES

After you write fortunes and mark different sections, your cootie-catcher becomes a fortune-teller. Write the name of a color on each of the four outer flaps. Open up the cootie-catcher, and write a number on each of the eight inner flaps. Then lift up each inner flap, and devise a fortune for each of the eight.

Now fold the fortune-teller back together, and spell out your fortune by moving your fingers and thumbs to expose different sections. Make one movement for each letter of the color you pick, as you spell it out. If you pick red, for instance, spell out *red* with a movement of your fingers for each letter, *R–E–D*. Then pick a number and move your fingers that many times. Pick another number and look under that flap for your fortune.

You don't have to stick with colors and numbers. Devise other labels. You could also write the names of people, animals, countries, cars, or anything else you like.

House of Cards

2 folded cards on flat surface

It's really hard to make a house of cards without using "the trick." You can try, but here's the trick. Fold two cards in half, and lay them on their sides so that they form a little box. If you try to make the house without these cards, it will be tough.

Lay another card across the top of these first two. Then make another little box on top of that with two cards folded, and then put

another card across that top. If you work on a flat surface and keep away from drafts, you can build your house of cards fairly tall.

After you become steady, play around building other structures, like two towers next to each other.

Some people consider it cheating to fold the cards, but it works for me. If you can find a way to stack them without folding them, that's great.

This is fun to do when you're sick, it's raining outside, or you're visiting relatives. Try it when your cousins ignore you or only want to talk about baseball.

Melon-Seed Necklace

Remember the melon seeds you dried for a melon-seed maraca? When you're done making music, you can use those same seeds to make a necklace. Just use needle and thread to string them. First, knot the end of the thread, Then pierce each seed with the needle and pull the thread through, to make a long string of seeds. When you've made this string the right length, tie the two ends together for a necklace.

Wear your necklace in its natural color, or paint the seeds with tempera poster paints. For a little variety, add shells to your melon-seed necklace. This could be a nice gift for your mom, aunt, or sister, or you could use it as buried treasure. You can also use other seeds, like winter squash, watermelon, or pumpkin for this seed necklace. Experiment.

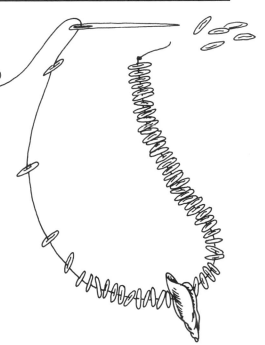

Papier-Mâché

Papier-mâché is French for "chewed-up paper." If you look at the glop you use to make it, you'll know why. First you make the papier-mâché; then you wrap it around something to create a shape. Have the object you want to wrap in papier-mâché ready first, then mix up the glop. Once you begin, you'll have glop on your hands, and you'll want to work quickly before it dries.

To create a round shape, wrap a balloon.

A tin can supplies the shape for lots of things, like animal sculptures, robots, or pencil holders. You can also wrap bottles to make bracelets or arm bands.

To create a free form, wrap papier-mâché around itself or scrunched newspapers. This would be great for painting or for Mexican piñatas that you could fill with small toys, candy, or party favors and decorate with streamers or tissue paper. Usually piñatas are shaped like animals, hung from the ceiling, while blindfolded guests take turns bashing the piñatas with a stick until they break and toys spill out.

If you want to remove dried papier-mâché from a base, you have to coat the base with petroleum jelly first. This works with balloons, cans, plastic, and cardboard containers, but it won't work with textured surfaces. If you wrap a balloon, you can also simply pop the balloon after the papier-mâché dries.

To prepare the papier-mâché, gather a bunch of old newspapers. Tear the newspaper into strips about 2 inches (5 cm) wide and 6 inches (15 cm) long.

Since making papier-mâché is pretty messy, lay down newspapers to work on and have a few more ready for the spot for letting your things dry.

Now you prepare the papier-mâché glop. Pour a cup of water into a bowl. Add a little flour to the water. Stir in a handful with your fingers until it makes a thin, gloppy paste.

Keep adding flour until it feels just right. You'll notice a floury, pasty smell, and your hands will be coated in an off-white layer of wet stuff. You'll be surprised at how much flour you'll need. So don't begin with too much water. If you goof and add too much flour, you can always add more water.

Here's the fun part. Pick up a newspaper strip and dunk it in the sticky flour-water paste. Push the strip under with your finger to make sure it's completely coated. Then pick it up and squeeze off the excess. You can slide two fingers along the strip and wipe the glop off.

This is your first papier-mâché strip. Place the strip on the object you want to cover and smooth it down. Tear the strip if it's too long. If it bulges, rip bits off to smooth the strip down over curves. Do the next strip. Just keep building up papier-mâché layers until you have a few thicknesses all over. Next, let your object dry. It will take several hours to dry.

You can paint your creation when it's completely dry. Take the papier-mâché off the base (if that's what you planned). Then paint, cut, or use it as part of another creation. You can make lots of things with papier-mâché.

MASK

Papier-mâché is great for making a mask. Cover half of a balloon with petroleum jelly and with papier-mâché. Prop the balloon between bowls or something else, or make a ring of masking tape on the balloon's bottom to secure it to the table. That way the balloon

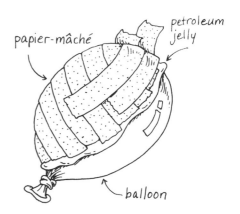

papier-mâché
petroleum jelly
balloon

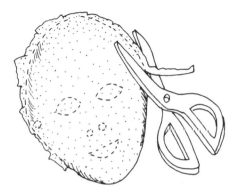

on each side of the mask to attach string and tie the mask onto your face. Or staple or tape a strip of balsa wood or strong cardboard to one side, and hold the mask to your face that way.

string for tying mask on

or attach a wood or cardboard holding stick

PAINT

won't roll all over from the weight of the papier-mâché while you work.

When the papier-mâché dries, pop the balloon, cut the mask's edges, and also cut out eyeholes so you can see and a mouth so you can talk and breathe. Paint on a base coat and facial features. Then, poke a hole

PENCIL HOLDER

Use an empty can with the top removed and no jagged edges left. You don't need petroleum jelly for this one. Wrap the entire can in papier-mâché,

including the top edge. When the papier-mâché is dry, paint it. Then fill the container with pencils or anything else.

ARM BANDS AND BRACELETS

A plastic soda pop bottle is the best thing to use as a base for an arm band or bracelet. Smear petroleum jelly all over the bottle's

widest part, and wrap papier-mâché around it.

After the papier-mâché dries, cut it in slices while it's still on the bottle. Thick

plastic soda pop bottle

papier-mâché

snip snip

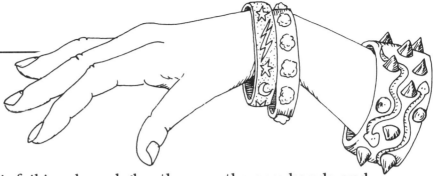

slices will produce arm bands. Thin slices will make bracelets. Then slip the plastic bottle out from under the papier-mâché.

Paint them all sorts of colors or even make fake tinfoil jewels and glue them on. Remember to wipe off the petroleum jelly inside the arm bands and bracelets before you put them on.

Potato Prints

cut potato in half

cut shape or design into flat side of potato

You can have fun a full morning or afternoon making potato prints. They're a little messy but not hard at all.

All you need is paper, paint, a knife, and a raw potato. Cut the potato in half, and then cut a shape or design into the flat half with your knife. When you have a design you like, dip it into the paint. Then press it onto paper, and your design will be printed on the paper.

The best paint to use is tempera poster paint. It's pretty thick, so pour a little onto a piece of cardboard or into the bottom of a plastic container. Or cut up an empty milk carton, wash it, and use it as a palette.

Don't forget that what you cut away will end up being the color of the paper, and what you leave sticking out will pick up the paint and print on the paper. This is like looking at a photograph negative that's the opposite of what it will end up looking like. Also, whatever you carve into the right side of the potato will come out on the

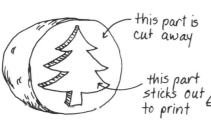

this part is cut away

this part sticks out to print

dip designed potato into paint

paint

flattened milk carton

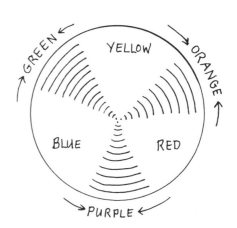

press potato onto paper to print

left side of the paper, and the other way around.

Use as many different cut potatoes and colors as you wish. Use a different potato for each color. Complete your design and let it dry. You could dry your prints by hanging them from paper clips or clothespins on a string tied between two chairs.

You can also print on fabric. Try potato prints on an old sheet, and then wrap it around you as a costume when it dries. Cut off the end of the sheet to use as a headdress. Also try printing your own special potato-print design on cut-up paper bags, and make them into book covers. Lots of people make cards from potato prints.

MIXING COLORS

When you mix blue and yellow you get green. If you print with red and then with blue right on top, you'll get purple. If you put red and blue and yellow together, you probably get a kind of muddy brown. Try mixing different colors to see what happens. If you're experimenting with color, you can try out food coloring and write down results of the different color combinations.

GREEN
YELLOW
ORANGE
BLUE
RED
PURPLE

Plaster of Paris

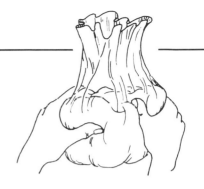

You'll need plaster of Paris, which you can buy cheaply at a hardware store. It is used for plastering walls, but artists also use it for sculpture. And you may have used it in art class.

Put a plastic bag in a big plastic bowl or other plastic container, and pour a cup of water into the bag. Begin sprinkling small handfuls of plaster of Paris into the water and letting it dissolve. Pretty soon, you'll see some floating on top and not dissolving. That means you've added enough plaster. You usually need twice as much plaster of Paris as water. So, for 1 cup of water, you'll probably need about 2 cups of plaster. And for 2 cups of water, you'll need about 4 cups of plaster.

Now, let the plaster begin to dry. As it dries, it becomes a little warm and hardens. After about 15 minutes you can begin to shape the plaster. Pick up the plastic bag and squish it around to make any shape you like. Just squish right through the plastic bag to shape the plaster.

You can also place objects in the plaster, like leaves or twigs sticking straight up or acorns and buttons set into the surface. If you make a boat shape, you can set in a twig as a mast. You can also make an impression of your hand or foot in the plaster as it dries, or draw a picture in it. Once it's dry, peel off the plastic bag and you have a nice paperweight or sculpture.

One thing to be careful about when you do this: Don't ever pour any plaster of Paris down the drain. It will clog the pipes and get

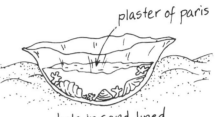

plaster of paris

hole in sand lined with plastic

you into big trouble. Just let it harden and then throw it away if you don't want it. If any gets into the bowl you used to hold the plastic bag, let that harden and then it will come right off the bowl. If you want to rinse out the bowl after that, do it outside.

Straw-Wrapper Spider

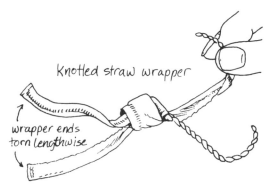

Knotted straw wrapper

wrapper ends torn lengthwise

If you have to sit still patiently, here's something fun to do. It will keep you busy while you're waiting for food in a restaurant.

Ask for a glass of water and a straw. Then carefully remove the straw wrapper. If you rip the wrapper the first time, ask for another straw and try again. Slide the wrapper off and flatten it out. Or you could rip a little off one end, scrunch the wrapper way down to the other end, and blow it off. Aim it somewhere harmless, like at an empty seat next to you or at the table right beside your glass. Otherwise, the waitress or your folks might take your straw before you've had a chance to make the spider.

Anyway, once you've flattened out the wrapper, carefully tie a loose knot in the middle. Avoid tearing the middle. Next, tear each end in half the long way— up to the middle between the crease and the wrapper seam. You'll have a knot with four long strips dangling from it.

Twist each strip between your fingers tightly all the way up to the knot. Sometimes it helps to lick your fingers a little, to get the twist started. But just a little, since it's important to keep the paper dry for now. Place your four-legged paper spider in a dry saucer, plate, or ashtray so that you don't get the table wet and get into trouble.

Dip the end of your straw in your water, press your finger over the top, and lift the straw out of the water. When you keep your finger pressed down, you create suction and water stays in your straw.

Now hold the end of the straw over the knot of your paper spider. Release your finger and the water in the straw. Wet the top of each spider leg. Watch the

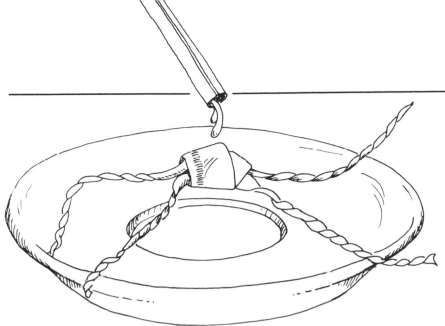

You can also make a straw-wrapper worm, if you scrunch the wrapper down when you take it off the straw. Wet the end, and when it "unscrunches" it will look like a crawling worm.

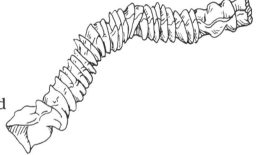

spider legs move as the water seeps through the paper to uncurl it. The spidery movements look creepy and real.

You may need to re-wet the legs a few times as the water is absorbed by the paper. Be careful not to get them too wet, or the paper will become a mushy mound instead of a creepy spider.

Walking on the Ceiling

This is something that may sound kind of silly, but if you try it you might want to make sure no one is around at first. You'll probably discover that it's really fun! Just clear a path.

Take a hand-held mirror, like a shaving mirror, and hold it under your chin, face up. Then look down into the mirror and start to walk slowly.

The mirror reflects the ceiling instead of the floor.

And soon you'll feel that you need to step over chandeliers and lintels (boards across the tops of doors and windows), ceiling fans, and whatever else is up there.

You also feel as though

so that only one side of your body is reflected in the mirror. The mirror will make it seem that both halves of your body are the same. Now, lift your arm and it will appear that both arms rise. Lift your leg, and you'll look like a puppet lifting both legs in the air at the same time. Doing jumping jacks with your reflection looks really neat.

walk all over the ceiling without falling off! This is especially fun in old houses with fancy chandeliers and plaster swirls.

Also try holding the mirror next to your face to reflect the wall next to you, and start walking. It really confuses you and you have no idea where you're going!

you can walk right through those things on the ceiling. You suddenly seem to have magical powers, like the Fly, Spiderman, or Superman. And you can

MIRROR IMAGE

Or try standing next to a full-length mirror (like one in a store dressing room)

Table Mischief

FLIPPING SPOONS

When you've finished eating, helped with the dishes, and aren't sure what you want to do, try flipping spoons. You'll want to clear the decks of any glassware or china first.

All you need is two spoons. Lay one spoon down with its bowl against the floor or table. Then rest the bowl of the second spoon on the handle end of the first spoon.

Now, bang your fist on the first spoon bowl's top edge. This will make the other spoon flip and fly into the air. See how far you can make it go or if you can make it do a somersault.

MYSTERIOUS BALANCING SALTSHAKER

Here's something to practice when you're alone, or just leave your masterpiece for someone to discover. Try this at a restaurant while you're waiting for food.

Pour a small pile of salt on the table or tablecloth and then settle the saltshaker on its bottom edge into the salt pile until it balances just right.

Then, the saltshaker will stand up by itself, but look like it's falling over. This works best with the little glass saltshakers with flat bottoms and sloping sides found in coffeeshops and diners.

Gently blow away some of the salt around the shaker, but just don't blow away the salt that holds it up. Then people won't have a clue about how you did the trick!

Simple Kitchen Experiments

SLOW-MOTION CORNSTARCH

If you haven't already done this in science class, try it. It sounds silly, but it's fun to watch.

Pour a little cornstarch into a small bowl or cup. Then add water and *slowly* stir it in with a spoon until you've added just the right amount of water to make a thick, gooey paste.

Here's the fun part. If

slowly stirring

you stir in slow motion, the cornstarch solution will stir like a liquid. But if you take the spoon and tap it fast into the cornstarch, the cornstarch suddenly becomes hard, and you won't be able to get the spoon into it. As long as you stir slowly, it behaves like a liquid, but when you try to move fast, the cornstarch acts like a solid. That's why I call this slow-motion cornstarch.

Add lots of water to clean the bowl, and then slowly stir the cornstarch out.

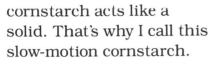

tap hard and fast with spoon to make cornstarch turn into a solid

BAKING SODA VOLCANO

vinegar foams as it flows down channels in baking soda

For a baking soda volcano, pour some baking soda into a dish in a pile, like a little mountain. Then, make a depression in the top with your finger. You now have a volcano shape.

To make it erupt, pour a little vinegar into the depression on top. A chemical reaction will immediately occur. The baking soda will foam like lava and pour down the sides of your kitchen volcano, just like a real, active volcano. When your volcano stops foaming, you'll find little craters.

You can make channels in the volcano's side to get the lava to run down where you want. You could make a chain of volcanoes, small ones and big ones, or draw a little town at the base of the volcano and watch the lava destroy the town. Or you could draw an island with blue ocean around it on a piece of cardboard. Then townspeople or islanders could escape by sea, using birch-bark boats.

LAVA BOTTLE

Pour some water and some vegetable oil into a clear bottle or jar with a lid. Then put the lid on tightly and agitate the oil and water a little. Watch what happens. The oil and water won't mix. They form a colloid. The oil separates into little beads that sit in the water. If you turn the bottle upside down, the oil beads float up through the water. Turn the jar right side up again and the oil

beads float through the water again, like a lava lamp.

Add a few drops of food coloring and see what happens. Some of the food coloring will mix with the oil bubbles and some will mix with the water. You'll see dark red (blue, green, or whatever color you choose) oil bubbles in light red (blue, green, or whatever) water. After a while all the food coloring will mix with the water. As it does so, the oil bubbles will look like exploding colors in the water. It's fun to watch!

colored oil drops floating in water

Fist Figures

FIST FACE

Make a fist, then move your thumb up just a little, and hold the thumb side towards you. The shape looks a lot like a funny face, with your thumb as the bottom lip and chin. Add eyes and big red lips with a pen, magic marker, or lipstick. Then, by swiveling your thumb knuckle up and down, the fist face will look as though it's talking.

Practice expressions by moving your hand and fingers in different ways. Then, add a goofy voice to make your fist face talk. Lay a handkerchief, tissue, or other covering on the top of your hand for its scarf or hair. This will also hide your wrist and arm.

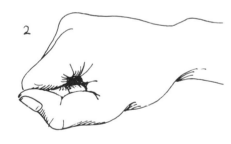

FIST PISTOL

You can make a water pistol out of your own hand. Try this when you're in the bathtub, or simply fill a sink with water. Make a fist, but instead of curling your fingers into your hand, lay the ends of your fingers flat against the heel of your hand. Press the fingers into your hand so that you can feel the suction pull your fingers into the palm of your hand. If you can't feel this, put your hand under water.

Get that suction going so that when you press your fingers into it, you'll suck out all the air from that space in your fist. Put your fist in the water. Now, when you release the pressure slightly, the space will fill up with water.

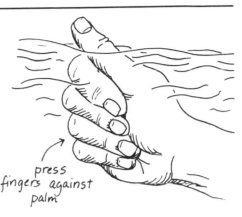

press fingers against palm

Hold your fist out of the water with your thumb side facing away from you. Move your thumb a tiny bit away from your first finger, to make a little hole. Then squeeze your fingers against your hand again, and the water inside will squirt out through that hole by your thumb. Got it?

Now aim and shoot. If you're at the bathroom sink and the mirror is steamy, you can draw a target on the mirror, and aim.

You can also do this when swimming.

Tub Boat

You can make a bathtub boat to sail in the tub, but you can also sail it outside on a pond, pool, or puddle.

It's easy to make a "tub boat." You need a piece of wood (balsa wood is easy to cut, but if it's too thin it will break), a milk or juice carton, and a rubber band.

Cut the wood into a boat shape like this.

Cut out two rectangles from the milk carton, both the same size. Make sure they'll fit between the two legs at the back of your boat.

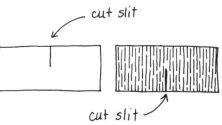

cut slit

cut slit

Fit the two rectangles together to make a propeller. You can do this by cutting a small slit in the middle of each one, only halfway across.

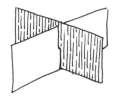

fit 2 rectangles together for propeller

Then, notch the outside of each leg.

balsa wood

cut notch

make rectangle size to fit boat

cut notch

Now stretch the rubber band across the legs of the boat, running it through the notches, and put the propeller in the rubber band as well.

To make your bathtub boat move, twist the rubber band around and around, turning the propeller with it, until it's tight. Then, place the boat in the water and let go of the propeller. The propeller will spin and the boat will zip across the tub. Twist the rubber band one way, and the boat will move forward. If you twist the other way, then the boat will move backward.

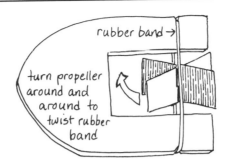
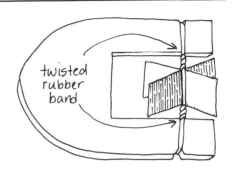

Shocking Stunts

WALL BALLOONS AND ZAPS

You can make an inflated balloon stick to the wall if you rub it gently on your arm first. This creates static electricity, which makes the balloon stick to the wall.

You can also build up static electricity if you scuff your feet on a carpet, especially in winter when the air is very dry, you know. You've been walking along, you suddenly touch something, and ZAP! You get a small shock. Put that energy to good use and make your finger into a zapper. Sometimes you can even see the shock. This kind of shock is not dangerous, but don't touch a computer since you may disturb its data.

HAIR-RAISING

If you have fine hair, you can do the same thing with a hairbrush. Brush your hair until static electricity builds up. After a while, your hair will cling to the brush, like metal attracted to a magnet.

Penny Soccer

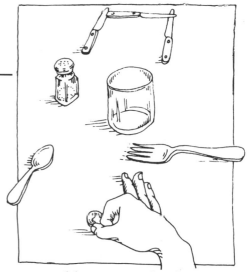

Penny soccer is best played on a smooth tabletop or floor. I used to play it on my desk at school, and it's also good to play if you're at the table waiting for everyone else to finish.

All you need is a smooth surface and a penny. You could also use a button if you don't have a penny. It's fun to have something to aim at, like three pencils or toothpicks or sticks set up to form a goal.

Set up your goal, place the penny on the table or floor across from it, then flick the penny with your index finger to make it shoot across. See how few flicks it takes to make a goal. You could set up an obstacle course and try to maneuver your penny around it. Salt and pepper shakers, spoons, erasers, pencil boxes, and other coins all make great obstacles.

When you get really good at this, try using your other hand!

Amazing Floating Wax Shapes

Get a glass of water. Put it on your work space. A kitchen table is a good spot.

Light a candle and hold it sideways so that the burning wick is over the glass of water. Allow the melting wax to drip into the water. The wax will float on the surface, and as soon as it hits the water, it will harden. Move the candle around a little to achieve different shapes. You could try using different colors of candles for interesting designs. It's also fun just to watch the wax drip onto the water's surface.

Because this involves a lighted candle, you'll want to have an extra glass of water and a grown-up nearby—just in case. Fire can be very dangerous.

If your grown-up says it's not okay to do this, try this instead. Get a glass of water, a toothpick, pencil, or stick, and food coloring. Put one drop of food coloring in the water, and swirl it around with the toothpick to make nice swirls. Then, use another drop of another color and swirl it around. You can make all sorts of beautiful designs with colors.

Sometimes the colors will swirl by themselves. If you swirl them too much with the toothpick, they'll all mix together in a muddy color.

If you dip a piece of paper into the water, it will pick up some of the colors. But you'll have to dip quickly before the colors mix together.

Paste Pictures

For paste pictures, you can collect all sorts of things—dried beans, uncooked macaroni, popped popcorn, pebbles, shells, buttons, leaves, acorns, yarn, twigs, or bits of eggshell. Then, make them into a design on a sheet of cardboard or paper. You could create a town for a baking soda volcano, with twig houses, button people, yarn streets, and cars with round macaroni wheels. You could also simply arrange the objects in a pretty pattern.

Paste the objects down on your drawing or create an abstract. Use white liquid glue or make your

floating wax

swirling colors

FOOD COLORS

own paste with a handful of flour mixed with a little water. Make it thicker than you would papier-mâché. This doesn't work as well as white liquid glue, but it's OK.

Dip your finger into a little paste, or use a small spoon, and smear it on the cardboard in a little mound. Then set a dried bean or another object firmly into the paste. It dries pretty quickly.

You can also first draw a design on the paper with the glue or paste, and sprinkle sand or glitter on the paper. The glitter or sand will stick to the glue but not to the rest of the paper. Tap the paper to remove the excess sand.

If you draw an outline of your hand with fingers spread, it makes a pretty fair turkey, nice for Thanksgiving. Paste dried

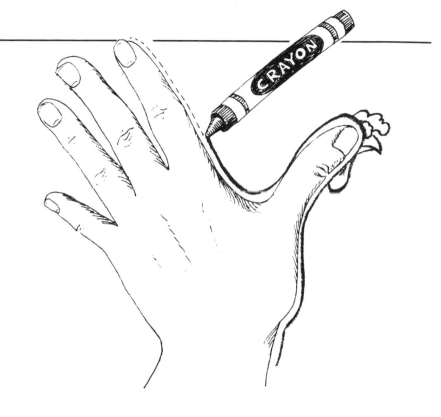

leaves and other stuff on the outline that look like feathers. Use a dried bean for an eye and tiny twigs for legs. A Cheerio also makes a good eye.

You could decorate a card-board box, like a shoe box or tea box, with fake jewels—tinfoil diamonds, split-pea emeralds, or lima-bean pearls. Use it to store melon-seed necklaces, papier-mâché arm bands, sea glass, and other treasures. Prepare one surface at a time so that it has time to dry. You could also decorate the cover of your Fantastic Voyage Logbook.

Flashlight Fun

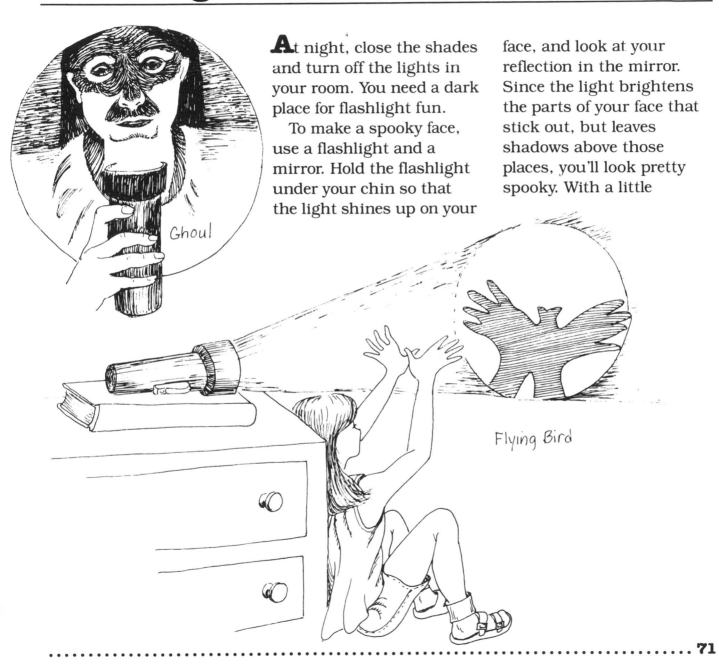

At night, close the shades and turn off the lights in your room. You need a dark place for flashlight fun.

To make a spooky face, use a flashlight and a mirror. Hold the flashlight under your chin so that the light shines up on your face, and look at your reflection in the mirror. Since the light brightens the parts of your face that stick out, but leaves shadows above those places, you'll look pretty spooky. With a little

Ghoul

Flying Bird

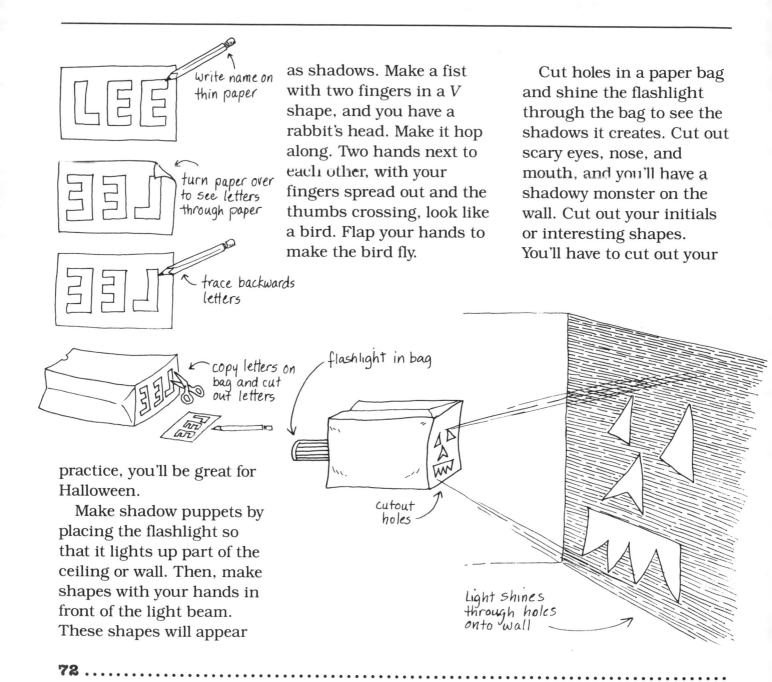

as shadows. Make a fist with two fingers in a *V* shape, and you have a rabbit's head. Make it hop along. Two hands next to each other, with your fingers spread out and the thumbs crossing, look like a bird. Flap your hands to make the bird fly.

Cut holes in a paper bag and shine the flashlight through the bag to see the shadows it creates. Cut out scary eyes, nose, and mouth, and you'll have a shadowy monster on the wall. Cut out your initials or interesting shapes. You'll have to cut out your

Write name on thin paper

turn paper over to see letters through paper

trace backwards letters

copy letters on bag and cut out letters

flashlight in bag

cutout holes

Light shines through holes onto wall

practice, you'll be great for Halloween.

Make shadow puppets by placing the flashlight so that it lights up part of the ceiling or wall. Then, make shapes with your hands in front of the light beam. These shapes will appear

initials backwards for them to look right on the wall.

Try writing them backwards first. Then, copy them when you cut out the bag. To write stuff backwards, write with very dark letters on a piece of thin paper, then turn the paper over and trace the lines to see what it looks like backwards.

Shine your flashlight on objects, like moths, to make them look really big. The closer the flashlight is to the moth, the bigger its shadow will be. Experiment. Since moths are attracted to light, if you wait by an open door or window long enough on a summer night, you may see one.

Button Games

press edge of first button down to flip second button

Collect as many buttons as you can, and, with a little imagination, you can play all sorts of games. Use buttons to outline the shapes or create pretty designs for pictures.

Toss the buttons into cups or at targets. Flick them with your fingers or flip them with another button. Different sizes or colors can represent armies or teams. You can stage great battles or hold a Button Olympics.

The game tiddlywinks involves flipping buttons. Press the edge of one button down onto the edge of a second button to make it jump. It takes a while to master this. If you press too hard, or the wrong way, the button might fly up into the air and land where it started. Or it might flip over and go in the wrong direction.

You could draw a target on the ground, mark your progress with sticks, or try to flip the buttons into a cup or a shell. Or simply see how far or how high you can flip your button.

Floating Arms and Stuck Fingers

Remember the character Thing, the hand that does all kinds of stuff by itself, on the Addams Family? Well, I can't tell you how to make such a hand, but I *can* tell you how to make your arms do something all by themselves.

Stand in a doorway, bend your arms, and then press them hard against each side of the door frame as long as you can. Try a full minute. When you can't do this anymore, relax your arms and let them fall gently to your sides. They'll soon start rising up all by themselves, as though they're floating. If you can't

press arms hard against door frame

let arms go; they'll rise by themselves

reach both sides of the doorway at the same time, do this with just one arm.

For a stuck finger, grab one of your fingers and grip it hard in your fist for about a minute. Then slide your finger out, keeping your fist in the same closed position, and lightly stroke the inside of your wrist for a few seconds. Now *slowly* try to open your hand, and your fingers will seem stuck closed. The only way to open your hand will be to do it quickly, all at once.

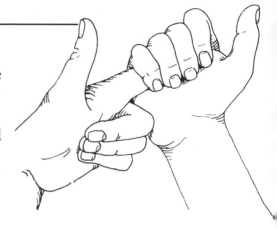

Fantastic Voyage Logbook

If you could go anywhere and be anyone in the world, where would you go and who would you be? In your imagination, you can go anywhere and be anyone you wish. Create a journal or logbook of your own fantastic journeys.

Find a notebook with blank pages, or use blank sheets of paper, punch holes in the side, and thread them together with yarn or string.

Then, you need lots of magazines and newspapers, scissors, paste or tape, and time alone.

Look through old magazines to find a picture of someone who can be *you*—the hero of your logbook. Or choose a photo of yourself or draw one. Paste that picture on the logbook's first page. Then find a picture of *where* you'd like to travel, and paste that in your log, too.

The rest is up to you. How will you get to your destination—by train, boat, or rocket? Who will you meet along the way? What towns and cities will you go through? What strange creatures will you see—lions and giraffes in Africa, sharks and octopuses in the bottom of the sea, Martians on Mars?

Find or draw pictures of all these things, and paste them in your book.

What will you do when you arrive? What will you eat, drink, and wear? Who will your friends be? What language will you speak and how do you say hello? Make up a greeting and write that in your book.

When you finish your journal or log, find a picture for the cover or glue on decorations. Also, make up a title, like "Queen Elizabeth of England: My Personal Diary" or "My Trip to the Bottom of the Sea." Put the log on your bookshelf to enjoy later.

You could create travel journals to all parts of the world and into space. You could also play many characters. You may actually see some of these places when you grow up. Who knows!

Time Capsule

What's your favorite thing to do? What's your favorite food? Who's your best friend? Do you have any enemies? What color is your hair? Is it curly or straight? How tall are you? Do you have any pets?

These things are easy to remember now, but in five, fifteen, or fifty years, you may not remember them so clearly. You could create a time capsule filled with things that describe who you are and save it so that you'll remember in coming years.

Find a shoe box or other box to keep everything in, and decorate it if you like. Write your full name and age on the box. Then, you're ready to fill it.

Begin with something that tells the date, like a newspaper or magazine page. Then maybe add a small lock of your hair and a baby tooth you've lost.

Inside your time capsule, you could put a photo of your best friend and write the friend's name on the back. Include a homework assignment you got a good grade on. Maybe a clean label or wrapper from your favorite food or drink. Perhaps a page from a television guide. Put in a sock or a lace from your sneakers.

List ten things you hate and make another list of ten things you love, and put that in, too.

Who's your favorite teacher? Which class do you like and which don't you like? What's your

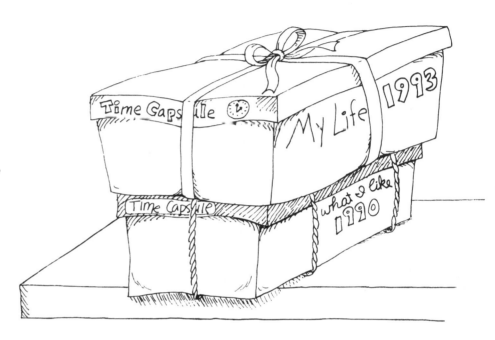

favorite book, movie, or song? Describe your pet, if you have one. Find a leaf or flower and press it.

You can put many things in your time capsule to remind yourself of who you are. When the box is full of things you've collected, put

on the cover, and tie it closed with a string, yarn, or ribbon. Then put it away. You can take it out whenever you like to see what's inside.

You could make a time capsule on your birthday or every few years.

Index